Somebody/Nobody

by Jane Martin

A SAMUEL FRENCH ACTING EDITION

SAMUEL FRENCH

FOUNDED 1830

NEW YORK HOLLYWOOD LONDON TORONTO

SAMUELFRENCH.COM

ISBN 978-0-573-66361-1   Printed in U.S.A.   #20723

MUSIC USE NOTE

Licensees are solely responsible for obtaining formal written permission from copyright owners to use copyrighted music in the performance of this play and are strongly cautioned to do so. If no such permission is obtained by the licensee, then the licensee must use only original music that the licensee owns and controls. Licensees are solely responsible and liable for all music clearances and shall indemnify the copyright owners of the play and their licensing agent, Samuel French, Inc., against any costs, expenses, losses and liabilities arising from the use of music by licensees.

**IMPORTANT BILLING AND CREDIT
REQUIREMENTS**

All producers of *SOMEBODY/NOBODY must* give credit to the Author of the Play in all programs distributed in connection with performances of the Play, and in all instances in which the title of the Play appears for the purposes of advertising, publicizing or otherwise exploiting the Play and/or a production. The name of the Author *must* appear on a separate line on which no other name appears, immediately following the title and *must* appear in size of type not less than fifty percent of the size of the title type.

SOMEBODY/NOBODY was first produced at the the Temple of Music and Art in Tuscon, Arizona on March 7, 2008. The performance was directed by Jon Jory, with sets by Matthew Smucker, costumes by Marcia Dixcy Jory, lighting by Michael Philippi, sound by Brian Jerome Peterson, fight direction by Ken Merckx. The Production Stage Manager was Bruno Ingram. The cast was as follows:

LOLI . . . . Jessica Martin

SHEENA. . . . . Alexandra Tavares

JOE DON. . . . . .Jeremy Stiles Holm

STALKER. . . . . .Claire Buchignani

GALAXY. . . . . .Elizabeth Gilbert

BEVERLY. . . . . Amy Kim Waschke

CHARACTERS

LOLI (Low-Li) – Small town girl with grit.

SHEENA – B-List movie goddess.

JOE DON – Survivalist and Bounty hunter.

STALKER – Vampire wannabe with orange hair.

GALAXY – B-List super agent.

BEVERLY – Graduate student.

TIMELINE

Act One, Scene One – 2PM

Act One, Scene Two – 6PM

Act Two – Next Morning

ACT ONE

Scene One

(A first floor studio apartment somewhere in working class Los Angeles. A barred window. We see a living room with an open kitchenette. Two doors, one to the outside, the other to the bedroom. A shag rug covers the living room floor. A small hooked rug lies on top of it near the worn sofa. Sparsely furnished, we also see a table with phone, a straight-backed chair, a bright colored beanbag chair, and an ancient standing lamp, from previous occupants. There is an ironing board and laundry basket, while above a Japanese lantern covers the ceiling fixture. The half kitchen has a microwave, two burner stove, fridge, and serving bar with a bar stool on the living room side. The walls are worn Spanish plaster and unadorned with the exception of a muddy work boot and a 2x4, both incongruously nailed up. The walls cease to be realistic toward the top. Behind them looms a large cutout of King Kong carrying Fay Wray and, partially obscured behind that, the iconic "Hollywood" sign. **LOLI,** *a young woman, glaringly average in every way, is crouched over the landline phone on the floor like an impassioned gargoyle. She struggles, internally, to snatch up the handset. Suddenly she stands up, arms extended.)*

LOLI. *(punches in phone number)* Doin' it, doin' it, doin' it, done. *(Someone answers.)* Oh Lord. Mr. Johnston? Hi, Mr. Johnston. I got your message. How I'm fired, that message. Loli. Me, I'm Loli. Please, please, please Mr. Johnston, don't fire me, please. L.A.'s real tough. Fixing those old pickups for you, that's pretty much the only job skill I got. I know you got a garage to run...yeah, three days, I know...I just...I wasn't myself Mr. Johnston, I was...shoot, I don't know what I was... Wait, Mr. Johnston, don't hang up, please don't, just let me...you hung up on me, you Pharisee!

(kicks phone) I am a terrible bad person! *(hugs her knees)* Why, why, why couldn't I get out of bed? *(phones rings)* *(suddenly grabs receiver)* Hello, Mama. Uh-huh. Yes, I know I'm a bad person. *(listens)* No, I am not coming home. Flatt, Kansas does not need me. Mama, you said nobody knew I'd left. *(hand over receiver)* Lord Jesus, earth's crown and hope, tear out my mama's voice box, tear it out. *(into phone)* Joe Don? You are not to send that devil's spawn to drag me back. You better stop him, Mama. 'Cause I am not coming back to Flatt, Kansas with my cousin the bounty hunter in his pickup with 17 bullet holes. Mama, he's got a human ear in a bottle on the dash.

*(wild pounding on **LOLI**'s door)*

Jesus wept. *(on phone)* Somebody is pounding on my door, that is why I said Jesus wept. *(pounding)* Who on earth is that?

SHEENA. *(off)* Help me. Let me in.

LOLI. Did you say "let me in"?

SHEENA. I'm hurt. Open the door.

LOLI. *(on phone)* There's a woman saying, "Help me, let me in."

SHEENA. I'll pay you a thousand dollars.

LOLI. *(into phone)* Get out of town.

SHEENA. Let me in!

LOLI. *(back on phone)* I'm going to open the door, Mama. No, I'm not using grandaddy's war pistol; it would blow me up. *(back to door)* Ma'am?

SHEENA. Do not call me, Ma'am.

LOLI. I got the chain on, so don't think you can do white slavery or steal my debit card. *(cracks the door)*

SHEENA. Let me in.

LOLI. Oh my Lord, oh my Lord, blood. *(closes the door, leans on wall)*

SHEENA. Let me in!

LOLI. Blood is a part of life. I can do this.

> *(**LOLI** throws the open door. **SHEENA**, a movie star beauty in her mid-twenties wearing a torn gold lame awards dress, her face a mask of blood enters the room like the Frankenstein monster. **LOLI** backs up and screams.)*

SHEENA. Let me out! *(She collapses.)*

LOLI. *(diving for phone)* She fell right down on the floor, Mama. I'll call 911.

SHEENA. *(sitting up)* Do you have a mango?

LOLI. Uh-uh.

SHEENA. Then I have to go.

LOLI. You are bloody like a hamburger. You can't go out.

SHEENA. They will send me back! *(tries to rise using sofa)*

LOLI. Back where?

SHEENA. To my life. Never mind, I'll commit suicide.

LOLI. No! No, no, no, you can't commit suicide here; it's a rental.

SHEENA. I'm going to be sick. I throw up when I see other people's blood.

LOLI. It's not other people's blood.

SHEENA. This is my precious blood?

LOLI. Pretty much.

SHEENA. Get this blood off me!

LOLI. Mama, I got to wipe off somebody's precious blood. Washcloth. *(Lays down phone. Goes to bathroom.)*

SHEENA. I can't stand this, I can't stand this.

LOLI. You can stand this, you can stand this.

SHEENA. Get this blood off of me so I can kill myself.

LOLI. *(returning with washcloth)* I'm just going to wipe, okay?

SHEENA. Ahhhh!

LOLI. Hold still.

SHEENA. Ahhhh!

LOLI. Just…

SHEENA. I go crazy when people hurt me…

LOLI. Yeah but…

SHEENA. I do, I completely freak.

LOLI. Just one wipe.

SHEENA. Fine.

LOLI. Good.

SHEENA. *(as* **LOLI** *carefully wipes)* No. No.

LOLI. Yes.

SHEENA. No.

LOLI. One more.

SHEENA. Ow.

LOLI. Just real easy. *(wipes)*

SHEENA. Ow.

LOLI. Uh-oh.

SHEENA. "Uh-oh" what?

LOLI. Well this is kind of a big old' cut.

SHEENA. On my face?

LOLI. Kind of up in your hair.

SHEENA. Yes! Yes! Up in my hair!

LOLI. It is.

SHEENA. A scar in Hollywood, that's your tombstone. Plus they can't ever again do work on my face due to Botox weakening the superstructure.

LOLI. Wow.

SHEENA. I could have a cave-in.

LOLI. Holy moly.

SHEENA. But up in the hair, I caught a break.

LOLI. That's right.

SHEENA. *(holds out her necklace)* My tooth has watched over me. *(suddenly aware of herself)*
There is blood on this dress.

LOLI. Well, yeah.

SHEENA. *(appalled)* Get me out of this dress. Get me out. Get me out of this dress.

(**LOLI** *moves toward her.*)

Wait. Get me a mauve silk robe cut above the knee with a belted tie in a contrasting color.

LOLI. A what?

SHEENA. Pure silk. I don't wear chemicals. Men get them on their hands when they undress you. And then the sex isn't organic.

LOLI. Ok, but I don't have a robe, I just go to bed nekked.

SHEENA. You may not see my flesh.

LOLI. You've got more flesh outside that dress then I ever saw on a person before.

SHEENA. That's public flesh. I am talking about my private flesh.

LOLI. Yubba.

SHEENA. And what the hell is "Yubba"?

LOLI. Well, when I was three I couldn't say "you bet" so I said…

SHEENA. Stop…chatting. A one hundred percent cotton sheet, have you got that?

LOLI. On my bed.

SHEENA. *(horrified)* A sheet you have slept on?

LOLI. You don't sleep on your sheets?

SHEENA. Do you have body lice?

LOLI. No, I don't have body lice; I am pretty damn clean!

SHEENA. Get the sheet!

(**LOLI** *goes to the bedroom.*)

Blood. Blood. Bodily fluids. *(tries to get out of dress)* Aaar-rggghh. *(Rushes to kitchen. Flings drawers open.)* I can't stand fluids on my clothes. *(Grabs a kitchen knife)* Off, off! *(tries to cut the dress off)*

LOLI. *(enters with a sheet)* Lord Jesus, don't kill yourself.

SHEENA. What is that?

LOLI. The sheet.

SHEENA. I cannot wear a sheet with duckies on it.

LOLI. I always had this sheet.

SHEENA. *(pulling at dress)* Get me out, get me out! I'm trapped in here. Get me out I'm claustrophobic.

LOLI. *(going to her)* I'm trying.

SHEENA. Hurry up.

LOLI. I'm hurrying.

SHEENA. It's eating me; it's a piranha dress.

LOLI. Wait, you got a zipper, right?

SHEENA. I don't know, do I?

LOLI. Well, how'd you get into it?

SHEENA. Are you out of your mind; I don't dress myself!

LOLI. Just turn around. Found the hook, I'll...

SHEENA. Unhook me.

LOLI. It's coming.

SHEENA. Sheet. Sheet!

LOLI. I only got two hands.

SHEENA. I'm cold; I'm cold! You're looking; you're looking!

LOLI. Do you want to be dressed or nekked?

SHEENA. You are touching me!

LOLI. Well, sheets don't just jump on you by themselves.

SHEENA. There are ducks; I don't like ducks.

LOLI. These ducks are all I got.

(As **LOLI** *gets the dress off,* **SHEENA** *ad libs, "no, no!" while covering herself with the sheet.)*

Yes! We did it.

SHEENA. Yes. Yes. There.

LOLI. I know you.

SHEENA. You do not know me.

LOLI. I do though.

SHEENA. Listen to me.

LOLI. What?

SHEENA. I want you to call my P.A.

LOLI. Sheena Keener.

SHEENA. No.

LOLI. *(fast, excited)* Sheena Keener, Sheena Keener, Sheena Keener.

SHEENA. I have never, ever heard of her.

LOLI. *(on phone)* Mama…a celebrity has descended into my apartment.

SHEENA. Call my P.A.!

LOLI. *(hand over receiver)* What's your Pa's number?

SHEENA. P.A., personal assistant.

LOLI. I never saw a celebrity with my own eyes.

SHEENA. Do not stare at me.

LOLI. I'm a big fan. I saw all three of your shark movies. You are fantastic when they eat you.

SHEENA. I know.

LOLI. I have all your CDs. I love your singing. It's so human how your voice cracks.

SHEENA. *(appalled)* How my voice cracks?

LOLI. You are the most famous entertainer of thirteen year-olds in the entire world.

SHEENA. Are you implying I have boundaries?

LOLI. Ummm…

SHEENA. I know no boundaries. I am limitless because I am like the ocean.

LOLI. Well, all right, but I have to pour hydrogen peroxide on your head first.

SHEENA. You are not pouring burning liquid into my brains.

LOLI. *(back on phone)* Mama, she won't use the peroxide; you think I could sew her up?

SHEENA. Give me that phone!

LOLI. Bye, Mama.

(Hands phone to **SHEENA.** *Going to the bathroom as* **SHEENA** *dials.)*

Will you, nil you, you got to be disinfected.

SHEENA. *(dials)* Priscilla? Oh, thank God, it's me. What do you mean "who," you're my personal assistant. Never mind where I am. Yes, I know the media is after me; it is your job to keep them off me. I'm just taking a little time off to be mentally unstable.

*(**LOLI** returns.)*

LOLI. *(establishing a comradeship)* I'm mentally unstable, too.

SHEENA. *(on phone)* What do you mean you have food poisoning? Priscilla, listen to me…

*(**LOLI** pours hydrogen peroxide on **SHEENA**'s cut.)*

Ow, Ow.

LOLI. Hold this clean cloth up to your head.

SHEENA. Ow. Get away from me. What do you treat, horses? *(on phone)* Priscilla…Priscilla…*(to **LOLI** who is approaching)* Back! *(on phone)* Priscilla you either get over here and get me to a safe place or…I cannot believe that! *(hands phone to **LOLI**)* Did that creepy little Canadian hang up on me?

LOLI. Well, unless she sounds like a dial tone.

SHEENA. *(grabbing phone)* You are so fired, Priscilla. *(hangs up)* She has betrayed me. Everyone betrays me. Okay, I have to stay here.

LOLI. Here? Here here? Like a pajama party?

SHEENA. No, not like a pajama party.

LOLI. But here in my house with me?

SHEENA. No, you should go somewhere else.

LOLI. Where?

SHEENA. How would I know…

LOLI. But I would like you to stay, I really, really, really would.

SHEENA. Fine. You sleep on the floor, you don't look at me, and you get me a sheet without ducks.

LOLI. Yubba.

SHEENA. And you don't say "yubba"!

LOLI. Yowsa!

SHEENA. God, I am so screwed up.

LOLI. You kinda are.

SHEENA. I didn't ask you.

LOLI. I'm kinda screwed up too.

SHEENA. Goddesses don't care about other people.

LOLI. Okay.

SHEENA. I have got to have a mango.

(Searches for the clutch purse she staggered in with.)

LOLI. A goddess. That's what you are.

SHEENA. I am. Yes.

LOLI. Could you teach me?

SHEENA. You? No. What are you talking about? You think it's easy being a goddess? A goddess pays; a goddess suffers.

LOLI. I just...

SHEENA. They devour you with their eyes. Everywhere the lust is palpable. Why can't I be left alone to be famous?

LOLI. Gollee. Don't cry Sheena Keener. You're a celebrity.

SHEENA. I fell down concrete stairs.

LOLI. I'm really sorry.

SHEENA. *(lifting sheet)* Look at my knees; look at them.

LOLI. They look really hurtful.

SHEENA. I was at the Surf Awards.

LOLI. I love awards. I love them with all my heart. They should have a special channel; awards, awards, awards every day.

SHEENA. *(looking down)* I never had bruises on my knees before.

LOLI. You are just all over beautiful.

SHEENA. I know. I used to be like you, but I stopped.

LOLI. How? How did you do that?

SHEENA. I erased myself and started over. What the hell is your name?

LOLI. Loli.

SHEENA. That is a sucky, sucky name. Don't say that name again.

LOLI. Only name I got.

SHEENA. Uh oh. Something bad is happening to me. Get me an unscented Kleenex.

LOLI. I got toilet paper. Toilet paper's soft.

SHEENA. When I'm dieting sometimes I eat toilet paper.

LOLI. You do not.

SHEENA. There's a place where movie stars can get it in flavors.

LOLI. Do they have cinnamon?

SHEENA. You looked at me.

LOLI. I forgot.

SHEENA. I cannot be looked at anymore; it is physically painful.

LOLI. Toilet paper. Band-aid.

(**LOLI** *goes to bathroom.*)

SHEENA. I have optiphobia: it's a neurological response to being seen. Eyes explode on me. They give little needle pains and I get an itchy rash where they look. My string bikini scenes are incredibly painful but it makes me writhe which is part of my charisma...

LOLI. *(returns with items)* I would like to be looked at.

SHEENA. No, you wouldn't.

LOLI. I'm invisible as a pane of glass.

SHEENA. *(getting band-aid out)* Well, I might as well have a target on my forehead. *(Tries to put it on. It falls off.)*

LOLI. You have to take the little papers off.

SHEENA. You do it.

(**LOLI** *gets down and puts band-aid on* **SHEENA**.)

I have a stalker, follows me all over the world.

LOLI. Wow.

SHEENA. She's a vampire from Berlin, Germany. She plans to drink my blood to become immortal.

LOLI. A vampire?!

SHEENA. And I saw her at the Surf Awards. She has orange hair and filed teeth.

LOLI. What's it like to get an award?

SHEENA. Hell on earth.

LOLI. That would be my dream. How you figger what to say?

SHEENA. You just thank all the people you hate, then you show cleavage and cry. Why are there bars on the window?

LOLI. Well...

SHEENA. This isn't an asylum is it?

LOLI. Huh-uh.

SHEENA. Good. *(looks at the window)* I have the most powerful B-list agent in Hollywood. She calls herself Galaxy because she is bigger than a star.

LOLI. Wow.

SHEENA. She is unbelievably dangerous and she is nineteen years-old.

LOLI. Really?

SHEENA. She is the prodigy of teen.

LOLI. Nineteen?

SHEENA. It's over at 23. Galaxy says I'm over-ripe, but I'm still very castable as food. She's got me signed to do this NASCAR horror movie about this cannibal race car. There's a scene in front of sixty thousand race fans where a Toyota eats me and then I'm excreted through the tailpipe.

LOLI. You're number one, though.

SHEENA. Maybe with sharks. Galaxy says any awards they give in the afternoon are nasty. I don't know, though; I won for "best partially clothed body devoured by a mechanical shark." *(fans herself wildly)* I have to do some compulsive eating. *(sees some fortune cookies left on a plate)* Fortune cookies!

LOLI. If you don't mind not eating those fortune cookies 'cause I've been saving them for when I need a really good fortune.

SHEENA. I'll just eat one. *(looks)* "You are the most beautiful woman who has ever lived."

LOLI. Shoot!

SHEENA. Huh, tell me something I don't know. *(shivers)* You see the stress I'm under?

LOLI. Yes, Ma'am.

SHEENA. I am not a ma'am. Do not call me a ma'am. Get out of my house.

LOLI. It's kinda not your house.

SHEENA. It is my house because I'm in it! *(hits herself)* That was bad. *(hits herself)* I know it's your house. I have to be kind to people homelier and less fortunate than myself. Anyway, I went up to get my Surf Award but I looked up and there were eyes, thousands of eyes, so I ran and I fell down a concrete stairwell, cut my head like you saw but I hitched a ride with a guy driving an ice-cream truck – boy did he drive fast – but he put his hand on me so when he turned down this off ramp I got the door open and rolled down this hill of jade plants. Then, I limped over to wherever this is, and here I am. What the hell is your name?

LOLI. Loli.

SHEENA. Still?

LOLI. Well, I…

SHEENA. Forget it. I need help; do you understand that?

LOLI. I will. I'll help.

SHEENA. You'll help me?

LOLI. Uh-huh.

SHEENA. You won't say you'll help me and then betray me?

LOLI. Huh-uh.

SHEENA. Something wonderful is going to happen to you now.

LOLI. It is?

SHEENA. I can't even describe it.

LOLI. Okay.

SHEENA. Kneel down.

LOLI. How come?

SHEENA. Because I told you to.

(**LOLI** *knees down.* **SHEENA.** *puts a hand on her head.*)

You are now my personal assistant, Priscilla.

LOLI. I am?

SHEENA. Yes.

LOLI. Oh my God, oh my God, I'm your assistant?

SHEENA. You are my assistant.

LOLI. Really?

SHEENA. Yes.

LOLI. I love that!! Yippee! Why am I Priscilla?

SHEENA. Because all my personal assistants are Priscilla. You are Priscilla the seventh.

LOLI. HOW come?

SHEENA. Because I like the name Priscilla. And here, here's your thousand dollars.

LOLI. In real money?

SHEENA. It's a little rank because I always tape cash to the bottom of my foot. My heels are the only things I never take off in public.

LOLI. Wow. I thought George Washington was on all the money.

SHEENA. Listen to me Priscilla! Look at me.

LOLI. You said not to.

(*makes her look*)

SHEENA. Do you see I'm shaking? I'm shaking my plastic surgery loose. It's liquefying. I'm melting due to being looked at. Would you want to melt?

LOLI. Huh-uh.

SHEENA. Nobody wants to melt. Nobody. That's why the *Wizard of Oz* is profound. Don't look at me.

LOLI. But you said…

SHEENA. I have to go live among primitive peoples who spend all day grubbing for roots with a sharp stick and then fall down exhausted and sleep. I read in *National Inquirer* there's a whole tribe that's gone blind from Nile fever. Don't you see how perfect that is? They would never, ever look at me, and I could, I don't know, take them downtown shopping or whatever.

LOLI. Uh-huh

SHEENA. It's a realistic plan; don't you think it's a realistic plan?

LOLI. Uh-huh.

SHEENA. Priscilla?

(**LOLI** *looks behind herself.*)

You're Priscilla.

LOLI. That's right.

SHEENA. It's hot. I'm boiling. Turn up the air.

LOLI. Don't have any.

SHEENA. Are you trying to cook me?! I raised my voice. *(hits herself)* Don't raise your voice. Priscilla, you have to save me. *(from her bag)* Take this card. That's my agency's address. Galaxy is suite one-thousand.

LOLI. One-thousand.

SHEENA. Go there.

LOLI. I'm not dressed too pretty.

SHEENA. Never mind. Say you are my new Priscilla. Cry or something. Can you cry?

LOLI. I cry all the time.

SHEENA. Say I am melting and have fled to…Abu Dhabi. Galaxy has a psychopathically short attention span. After three days she'll write me off. Then we can go to the Amazon where no one would look at me and I'll be saved.

LOLI. I would go to the Amazon?

SHEENA. You said you'd help me.

LOLI. *(Hugs her.* **SHEENA** *is stiff as a board.)* I go to this address.

SHEENA. Yes.

LOLI. I say I'm your assistant.

SHEENA. Yes.

LOLI. Suite one thousand. Galaxy, bigger than a star.

SHEENA. Yes.

LOLI. You went to…

SHEENA. Abu Dhabi.

LOLI. Then I come back.

SHEENA. Yes.

LOLI. Is it too far to walk?

SHEENA. You have a thousand dollars. You take a cab.

LOLI. Wow.

SHEENA. My life is in your hands. Feel my heart.

LOLI. *(touches her chest)* I feel your beating heart. I can do this.

SHEENA. You can?

LOLI. I can.

SHEENA. Maybe I like you. I have to sleep now. *(She collapses on the floor.)*

LOLI. *(looking down)* You must be pretty tired, huh? *(a moment)* You aren't dead are you? I don't want to be electrified. *(bends over)* No, you're breathing alright. That sheet's pretty thin. *(gets afghan off sofa)* My mama made this afghan; it's a tad ugly, but it's warm.

(Covers her up. **SHEENA** *speaks her dreams.)*

SHEENA. Bugs. Bugs. Don't lay your eggs inside my skin.

LOLI. I don't think we're really going to the Amazon. *(hugs herself)* I turned into Priscilla, I got a movie star on the floor, and I'm gonna ride in a cab. *(goes to door)* Like my Mama says, 'every frog has his day.'

*(***LOLI*** *exits. A moment.)*

SHEENA. *(fighting off a nightmare in her sleep)* Don't take me to your hive.

(Sleeps again. Sound of door being jimmied. A man enters. Stands. **SHEENA** *makes sounds in her sleep. The man moves dawn and gingerly pulls away the afghan.)*

Off. OFF!

MAN. Well. Look what the cat drug in.

(blackout)

End of Scene One

Scene Two

*(It's late afternoon. **SHEENA** still sleeps. A key in the lock. **LOLI** enters. She is euphoric. She carries a mango.)*

LOLI. Yes! Oh yes! Hey, Miss Keener…*(puts mango down)* You still taking a nap, huh? *(gently in her ear)* Hey, Miss Keener….

*(**SHEENA** deep in a nightmare, screams.)*

Good Lord, my heart.

SHEENA. Keep that Toyota away from me!

LOLI. It's alright.

SHEENA. No, no, no, no….

LOLI. Steady down now, whoa, Nellie.

SHEENA. Is this hell?

LOLI. Well, it's greater Los Angeles.

SHEENA. Who are you?

LOLI. I'm your personal assistant.

SHEENA. Fine. Get me a Swedish effervescent water.

LOLI. Only got tap or Big Red.

SHEENA. Big Red?

LOLI. Well it's kind of a fruit drink several times removed.

SHEENA. Are there bugs in my hair? Get them off! Get them off!

LOLI. No bugs, Miss Keener!

SHEENA. Do not call me that. They call washed up stars "Miss" this and "Miss" that and I am still rocking out.

LOLI. What should I call you then?

SHEENA. If it's professional or you're a fan you call me Sheena. Otherwise you call me Crackly.

LOLI. How come Crackly?

SHEENA. Because my bones crackle like rice crispies when you have sex with me.

LOLI. Oh. Me?

SHEENA. No, not you. No one would have sex with you. Now get me this Big Red thing and six ounces of spicy kelp.

LOLI. What's kelp?

SHEENA. Kelp is the source, the center. My God, what do you eat?

LOLI. Well, I could rustle up some buttermilk flapjacks.

SHEENA. Fine. Feed me. And get me something couture to wear.

LOLI. I got overalls.

(goes to laundry basket by the ironing board)

SHEENA. Fine !

LOLI. *(going through basket)* With maybe my antique Dolly Parton T-shirt.

SHEENA. *(a thought)* Wait a minute.

LOLI. *(pulling overalls and shirt out of basket)* Got 'em!

SHEENA. Wait a minute, wait a minute.

LOLI. *(coming to her)* It's all ironed.

SHEENA. You're Priscilla. *(phone rings)* I sent you on an errand.

*(**LOLI** picks it up.)*

LOLI. I did it real good. *(into phone)* Just hold your horses, Mama.

SHEENA. And?

LOLI. I came back. *(hands over receiver)*

SHEENA. Tell me…what…happened?!

LOLI. *(putting receiver down)* Well I rode in a real good cab with a honeysuckle air-freshener…

SHEENA. At the agency.

LOLI. Yubba. Well, it has this brass revolving door out front…

*(**SHEENA** puts on the clothes.)*

I went around a whole bunch before I got the hang of it.

SHEENA. And you told Galaxy what?

LOLI. Okay, suite one thousand. Now, I went in where you wait...kinda stood on the edge of it cause I didn't want to put my dirty shoes on that Chinese rug. But finally I just yelled out "Sheena Keener's gone to Abu Dhabi!", and boy, all hell broke loose...this alarm bell went off, people whanged out of doors and these vituperous Dachshunds got loose, went after the reception lady. Boy, she vaulted over her counter thing but she knocked over this espresso set-up which spilled on this dandy man's white linen suit and he lets out this yell and his chair tipped over backwards so his cigar set these skinny curtains on fire which set off some sprinkler things and then bam! This young girl with these murderous eyes comes out this golden door, and all these wet people backed up against the wall...shoot, even the Dachshunds backed up and she walked up real, real close to me and says, kinda sweet and poisonous, did I know who Louis the Fourteenth was? And I did, I studied that. And she said she was the Louis the Fourteenth of Hollywood, her name being Galaxy-bigger-than-a-star. So I went into Abu Dhabi real strong and she asked who it was I figured I was? So I said I was Priscilla the seventh, your personal assistant and she said...giving me the death eye...that if you had run off she would flay me alive, and she claps her hands and this Dachshund launches at me but I duck and it lands on her, and while the two of them go at it like the lions and Christians, I ran down seventeen flights of stairs and got me a cab ride back and here I am. Oh. Stopped off on the way home and got you a mango.

(produces it)

SHEENA. That was very, very good Priscilla. *(takes it)*

LOLI. Boy, I tried hard.

SHEENA. And they didn't follow you? You weren't followed?

LOLI. I ran six blocks before I took the cab.

SHEENA. That is so good! Here, you can have my used lipstick.

LOLI. Oh my God!

SHEENA. Now we wait three days. Then I disappear into the rainforest.

LOLI. See, I'm not sure that's a real nice place.

SHEENA. Flapjacks.

LOLI. I can do 'er. *(heads for kitchen)*

SHEENA. *(stopped by the wall decorations)* Why do you have a boot and a stick of wood nailed to the wall?

LOLI. *(working in kitchen on flapjacks)* Okay. Well, down in Flatt, Kansas where I come from...

SHEENA. It's flat?

LOLI. *(in agreement)* Where I come from.

SHEENA. *(getting knife to peel mango)* It's flat where you come from?

LOLI. Flatt! Oh, I get it. Capital "F" L-A-T-T. See Flatt's the town's name and not what you think, not because it's... *(gesture)* Flat. The town's two "T", Flatt. *(gesture)* Not flat, one "T".

SHEENA. I don't know if I can spend three days with you.

LOLI. See Flatt's, two T's, named after Jacob Flatt who crossed the great plains barefoot pushing a hand cart 'til he got mired in a blizzard and his toes fell off with frostbite.

SHEENA. His toes?

LOLI. Some say he got so bad he had to eat 'em in a soup.

SHEENA. Shut up!

LOLI. But anyhow, he pulled a chair off his hand cart, sat right down on it and started a town. Which explains Flatt, not... *(gesture)*

SHEENA. I would never eat my toes; I'm vegan. *(eats the mango)*

LOLI. Okay. But see, the 2x4, my brother Jomo, he laid out the football coach with that. Other one's my deceased brother Joeboy's workboot got thrown some distance from his pickup when he hit the storm tree going too fast on the "murder curve." Unfortunately his foot was in it. I don't mean now.

(**SHEENA** *puts her head in her hands.*)

LOLI. *(cont.)* Anyway, there's just not much doing in Flatt, so those boys get hammered and do dares on that curve…they hit the storm tree.

SHEENA. That is so real.

LOLI. Yeah. I sit here some nights and cry over that boot.

SHEENA. That is so sad. *(struck)* You are a human being. You mind if I touch the boot?

LOLI. No, you go right on. *(She does.)*

SHEENA. Makes me wish my brother was dead.

LOLI. *(suddenly)* Oh my Lord, I left Mama on the phone all this time. Mama? Oh shoot, I woke you up, huh? I'm sorry. Well, I got stuff on the stove and I'm hanging up so Joe Don can get through and you can call him off. Bye. *(hangs up)*

SHEENA. I thought he died?

LOLI. Joe Don? Oh, I see…he's not Joeboy or Jomo my brothers, he's Joe Don my cousin, the survivalist and bounty hunter. Joeboy's the one got decapitated by the storm tree. *(busy with flapjacks)*

SHEENA. Priscilla, your tragic background has touched me. It has. You know what? I want you to have these leopard bone earrings right off my ears. *(takes them off)* They were given to me by a shaman I recently slept with. He says you can find underground wells with them. I won't need them because they'll already have water when I get to the Amazon.

LOLI. See you have everything and you want out, and I haven't got anything and I want in.

SHEENA. In where?

LOLI. Won't be a soul knows I was ever here. People see you. They know you're here because you're beautiful.

SHEENA. Being beautiful just pisses everybody off, Priscilla. You have kick-ass style. Real edgy. Bold but clean.

LOLI. I just nailed that boot up.

SHEENA. But that's it. *(looks around)* All this. It's edgy, like poverty. *(calculates)* What's this little red table?

LOLI. It's a fruit crate. I just sprayed it red.

SHEENA. That is so beast! I might put out a furniture line like this. Pre-stained with indeterminate fluids.

LOLI. *(touching the boot)* Wow, I love that! I'm never going back.

SHEENA. Back where?

LOLI. Kansas.

SHEENA. What is Kansas?

LOLI. It's the big empty. *(sits on beanbag chair)*

SHEENA. I would like to be someplace empty. Is it lonely?

LOLI. Yeah.

SHEENA. What's the loneliest part?

LOLI. To go far out and sit in the corn.

SHEENA. Corn is on stalk things, right?

LOLI. *(nodding)* Stalk things.

SHEENA. *(sits with **LOLI**)* Can they find you in the corn?

*(**LOLI** shakes her head.)*

And nobody cares?

*(**LOLI** shakes her head.)*

That's how I'd like to think about Heaven. You just sit there on a cloud for a thousand years and nobody comes by. Pet me.

*(**SHEENA** lies head on **LOLI**'s lap.)*

LOLI. This one time my daddy made me this mountain so I could see over the corn. Bulldozed these cow pies, real high and stuck this old yellow kitchen chair up there so I could see out far. Said to me, "There you go girl, you got your own personal Heaven." Then he drove off to get us some fudge ripple. Sitting on that chair I could see his old Dodge kicking up dust all the way to the fence line. He never came back though.

SHEENA. That's generally what men do. I keep replacement men in my extra bedrooms. Corn girl in L.A.…What on earth is the point of you in L.A.?

LOLI. Boy, I don't know.

SHEENA. You have a job?

LOLI. I'm still Priscilla the seventh, right?

SHEENA. Before that.

LOLI. Well, I got on at the Pasa Robles Garage fixing gardeners' old pickup trucks.

SHEENA. *(horrified)* With your hands? I wouldn't like to touch things with my hands.

LOLI. My brothers taught me because it was all they knew to know. My whole life I fixed trucks.

(The timer for pancakes goes off.)

SHEENA. Do you have hand cream?

LOLI. Over by the phone. You know how all the gardeners out here drive those junky pickups? We got five mechanics can fix the computer chip cars but those old gardener trucks I'm the oneliest one.

SHEENA. That is more food than I ever saw on a plate.

LOLI. You just tuck that in.

SHEENA. You are a strange chick. Do you have a life?

LOLI. Not to speak off.

SHEENA. How many boyfriends are you jacking?

LOLI. Guess I kinda had one.

SHEENA. Total?

LOLI. Yeah.

SHEENA. One is not a total. Most nuns do better than that. One boyfriend, that makes me sad.

LOLI. Well, he was Joseph "Aces High" Cardwell, Flatt's only policeman. He turned into my boyfriend on his fiftieth birthday when I gave him a cupcake with a candle in it and he pulled me into the back seat of his cruiser.

SHEENA. *(half listening as she looks over the apartment)* Cruiser sounds good.

LOLI. He never spoke to me after that.

SHEENA. I don't like it when boyfriends talk. *(picking up a framed photo)* Is this little girl holding hands you?

LOLI. *(evasive)* Probably.

SHEENA. Who's that cute boy?

LOLI. *(taking it)* Never you mind that.

SHEENA. *(reacting to her snarky tone)* Listen to you. Have you ever seen a play Priscilla?

LOLI. Stage play?

SHEENA. That people watch?

LOLI. I was in my senior class play dressed as half a dog.

SHEENA. My agent says I have to do a play because there are rumors I'm animated. *(pinches herself)* I'm real. It is Romeo and Juliet which was originally a ballet but now there's a stage version. Being in a play is scary, right?

LOLI. Well, more if you weren't inside a dog.

SHEENA. All those eyes. *(shudders)* I'm not doing that. Galaxy made it sound good, too. Juliet's name is right in the title. My last movie only the shark's name was in the title. It was "Shark III!" with an exclamation point.

LOLI. *(excited)* But you had your own name in a title, right? "Sheena of the Jungle!"

SHEENA. That is not my favorite movie. I hope you didn't see that one.

LOLI. They wouldn't let it into Flatt. I heard about it in a sermon though. Boy, you get seen in the movies, you have a glorious life. My life, I get fired because I couldn't get out of bed.

SHEENA. I can't get out of bed. I have seven alarm clocks.

LOLI. Why can't I get out of bed?!

SHEENA. See, that's it!

LOLI. It is.

SHEENA. You can't get out of bed, neither can I. We get the shakes and we can't do it.

LOLI. We can't!

SHEENA. I'm a goddess, Priscilla...

LOLI. You are!

SHEENA. And if a goddess has no reason to get out of bed... *(crosses to counter)* I might as well... *(picks up small butter knife)* I don't know what...

(JOE DON enters behind her.)

Stab myself through the heart with...whatever this is...

LOLI. A butter knife.

SHEENA. A butter knife!

(JOE DON grabs her hand and bangs it on the counter until she drops it.)

Aaaaaah!

JOE DON. Beg your pardon but I had to save your life.

LOLI. Joe Don!

JOE DON. Loli Elizabeth.

SHEENA. *(whacking him)* Do not ever touch me.

JOE DON. No disrespect intended.

LOLI. You miserable piss-ant, what are you doin' in here?

JOE DON. Just catchin' forty. You put me to a hell of a long drive, girl.

LOLI. So you just broke in?

JOE DON. Cheap lock. *(takes her by the wrist)* Your mama's waitin' on you.

LOLI. *(resisting)* I am staying here.

JOE DON. Not in the cards, girl. *(moving her toward the door)*

SHEENA. Stop right there.

JOE DON. *(pleasantly, but still holding LOLI)* Little darlin', this here's my cousin. *(starts off with her)*

SHEENA. Do not mess with my personal assistant!

(leaps onto JOE DON's back)

JOE DON. What the...who we got here Loli?

LOLI. That's Sheena Keener up there.

JOE DON. Well, she oughta come down and say hello.

(Reaches up, grabs **SHEENA** *by the hair, pulls her off so she's back on the beanbag.)*

SHEENA. Murder, rape!

JOE DON. Ma'am, I just removed you offa my back.

SHEENA. Do not call me ma'am!

JOE DON. Well sugar, let me give you a hand up.

SHEENA. Leave me alone, leave me alone, leave me alone.

(She curls up into a fetal position.)

JOE DON. What's she doin' now?

LOLI. I don't know what that is. Joe Don…

JOE DON. Loli Elizabeth.

LOLI. I called Mama and told her to call you off.

JOE DON. Just a little family reunion.

LOLI. You came two thousand miles, Joe Don.

JOE DON. Weather was nice. I could value a cup of coffee.

LOLI. I will give you a cup of coffee but I am not going back to Flatt.

JOE DON. *(pleasant)* Go or be taken.

LOLI. No I will not!

*(**LOLI***'s forcefulness brings* **SHEENA** *fiercely to a sitting position.)*

SHEENA. Arrrrrrrgahhh! *(folds immediately back asleep)*

JOE DON. She's a pistol, isn't she?

LOLI. *(going to kitchen)* One cup.

JOE DON. *(picking up framed photo on the kitchen island)* This here you and me?

LOLI. Take it black, right?

JOE DON. You and me in our bathing suits.

LOLI. I was nine, you were grown.

JOE DON. Your daddy's home.

LOLI. What?! She let that shiftless, run-off, no account man back in the house?

JOE DON. He's got the cancer pretty bad.

LOLI. Mama's got no business to take him in.

JOE DON. You got to turn him every couple of hours like a roast.

LOLI. Well, that's just terrible but she doesn't owe him nose boogies.

JOE DON. You know your mama.

LOLI. All this time I figured he died.

JOE DON. No, he came home. *(picks up* **LOLI***'s last fortune cookie)*

LOLI. Do not eat my last fortune cookie.

JOE DON. You kind of wound up, girl.

> *(***LOLI*** *takes the plate.* **JOE DON** *points at wall.)*

Is that Joeboy's boot?

LOLI. *(bringing coffee)* It is. Now suck this and split.

JOE DON. I cut down that damn storm tree, took me three chainsaws. That old tree coming down, it screamed like a human child.

LOLI. Drink up.

JOE DON. Loli, she needs a hand with your daddy.

LOLI. You're a second cousin Joe Don; it's none of your beeswax.

JOE DON. Come hell or high water that dude is family.

LOLI. Family? Joe Don you are solitary as a hawk. You might as well be a sasquatch. Up some un-climbable cliff in Arkansas, snowed in all winter. No phone. Doin' that appendectomy on yourself with a pocket knife?

JOE DON. It was exploratory.

LOLI. How'd Mama get hold of you anyways?

JOE DON. Your mama sent the sheriff up in his helicopter. I do some bail jumpers for him.

LOLI. So now the bounty's on me, huh?

JOE DON. You're a home girl Loli Elizabeth. Not right for Sodom and Gomorrah.

LOLI. Did you just talk Bible? I've seen you go through all seven sins in twenty-four hours! You served three months for cutting off some stranger's ear in a bar fight.

JOE DON. Sonofabitch ordered Danish beer.

LOLI. Joe Don! You don't do a damn thing in the world but what you want. Now what I want is to stay right here. My life just took off, Joe Don. I got a celebrity roommate who won a Surf Award.

JOE DON. What the hell is a Surf Award?

LOLI. And just how would I explain that to a man lives off the map in a broke-down cabin, eats frogs and spiders?

JOE DON. I eat like a damn duke up there.

LOLI. If a duke eats raw thigh of raccoon.

JOE DON. You don't eat a raccoon raw. You've got to simmer slowly, add paprika, then dry, braise, drain, and brown lightly. Remove with a slotted spoon and serve over wild rice on a bed of artichoke hearts and then overspoon a choke-berry reduction.

LOLI. How many human beings you see in a year Joe Don?

JOE DON. I don't know. Two.

LOLI. Then don't carry on like you understand 'em. Go back to Flatt? You remember our housefire? I was the only one nobody remembered to bring out. Heck, Joeboy even brought out the ant farm, I was out...and nobody remembered that either.

JOE DON. There's always mistakes made in a fire.

LOLI. Whereas here, Hollywood, California, I rocketed all the way up to personal assistant. Like a meteor, that fast.

JOE DON. Your mom took me in for a year when I run off, and I have given her my word...my sworn word I would fetch you.

LOLI. You swore you would come back and take me to the prom if I didn't have a date too. What happened to that?

JOE DON. *(running a comb through his hair)* Now Loli, if I swore I would stuff you with poppin' corn and roast you on a spit 'til you sounded like a motorcycle, that is what I would do.

LOLI. No way.

JOE DON. Easy or hard, I'm taking you home.

LOLI. Huh-uh.

JOE DON. Hell I'm not.

LOLI. *(screams, points behind him)* Look out!

(He looks, she races into the bedroom. By the time he gets there she has locked the door.)

JOE DON. *(pulls handle, kicks door in frustration)* Girl, I will break it down.

LOLI. And I will shoot you with Grandaddy's war pistol.

JOE DON. Loli, that thing don't work...

*(**LOLI** from the inside fires a shot through the door that goes over his head. Splinters fly.)*

Usually.

SHEENA. *(startled into consciousness)* Bugs! Bugs.

JOE DON. Will you stop doing that?

LOLI. *(off)* Next time I won't aim high.

SHEENA. Who are you?

JOE DON. Did you see me fall for that? *(stares at ceiling)* I cannot believe I fell for that. *(yells toward bedroom door)* I could kick in that damn door and wrap that old pistol around your neck but I'm just sick of myself. *(yells again)* Drove 2000 miles to get shot at! *(calming down)* Do you want some coffee, Ma'am?

SHEENA. Do not call me Ma'am!

JOE DON. *(pours for himself)* I'd get off that floor girl.

SHEENA. Why?

JOE DON. 'Cause there's cockroaches crawling up your overalls.

*(**SHEENA** screams, she frantically whacks at herself and the sheet.)*

SHEENA. Is it off me? Get them off me!

JOE DON. *(a radiant smile)* Just kiddin'.

SHEENA. Creepy, half-witted hick.

JOE DON. *(smiling)* You pronounce that Joe Don, ma'am.

SHEENA. Get out.

JOE DON. Just poured my coffee.

SHEENA. It has been told you, and told you not to call me ma'am.

JOE DON. Well ma'am, you are a ma'am, ma'am, so I got to call you ma'am.

SHEENA. I'm twenty-two years-old and the most heartbreakingly delicate, beautiful thing you ever saw or could hope to see in your miserable, illiterate, in-bred life and you will obey me. Now get me a mango.

JOE DON. What the hell's a mango?

SHEENA. Are you insane?

JOE DON. *(looks her over)* Listen, I got to say if you're twenty-two you got some hard wear on you ma'am.

SHEENA. I can't believe you said that.

JOE DON. Well, when the bar closes, a good looking female's any age she wants to be.

SHEENA. Is it possible you don't know who I am?

JOE DON. Only friend I ever saw Loli have.

SHEENA. I am Sheena Keener.

JOE DON. Joe Don Carfleck.

SHEENA. Excuse me. Excuse me. I don't care who you are. I am Sheena Keener.

JOE DON. Joe Don Carfleck.

SHEENA. *(pounds her chest in frustration)* Sheena Keener!

JOE DON. *(amiably pounds his own chest)* Joe Don Carfleck. *(chuckles)* You're a helluva lot of fun.

SHEENA. I am Sheena Keener! I am in the movies!

JOE DON. See Sheila...

SHEENA. Sheena.

JOE DON. These people seen you in the movies and so forth, who are they you should give a rat's ass? What I seen of 'em, human beings is the scum of the earth, self-serving, selfish, oafish, money grubbin', brainless idiots. Hell they don't deserve to touch the hem of your garment. See, if I had my finger on the button Sheila, I'd eradicate 'em in a heartbeat.

SHEENA. I-am-not-Sheila.

JOE DON. Well girl, you be whatever you want to be. But when swine looks at pearls, they turn those pearls into swine. Me, I just live where the swine don't root. I'm shut of 'em. I live alone in nature's cathedral. You were in my charge little lady, I wouldn't let them look at you.

SHEENA. Really?

JOE DON. Guaranteed.

SHEENA. Really?

JOE DON. Done deal, take it off the table!

(*A moment and then* **SHEENA** *shoots into his arms and kisses him hard.*)

Seems a little premature.

SHEENA. You like women Joe Don?

JOE DON. Long as they're gone in the mornin'!

SHEENA. Every time?

JOE DON. Historically.

SHEENA. Pour me a cup of coffee.

JOE DON. Well, I believe I'll do that.

SHEENA. (*as he pours*) I hate just about everybody.

JOE DON. Good choice.

SHEENA. I do.

JOE DON. I run the table on that one. Six ball in the corner pocket.

SHEENA. Strange dude. (*hands her the coffee*) What are you Joe Don?

JOE DON. Nihilist. See, I...Listen here, I have a real hard time talkin' serious to a woman in a Dolly Parton T-shirt. I got my second best shirt in my bag. (*pulls it out*) Put it on. (*tosses it to her*)

SHEENA. I never wore someone's else's shirt until today.

(She smells it.)

JOE DON. Well, it's a hell of an experience. *(He turns around, leaning one hand on a wall.)*

SHEENA. What do you hate the most about people?

JOE DON. Maybe how they breathe, how their chests go in and out.

SHEENA. Yea, that bites.

JOE DON. Yeah.

SHEENA. Their stupid ears sticking out.

JOE DON. Well, you can cut off ears.

SHEENA. But what I really hate is their eyes.

JOE DON. The way they blink. I don't like that.

SHEENA. Moist, bulgy with those red veins.

JOE DON. Yeah, those veins suck.

SHEENA. Those eyes burn me like dead souls in hell fire.

JOE DON. Excuse my saying so, but that's real poetic.

SHEENA. Is it?

JOE DON. Yeah. You mind if I say something personal?

SHEENA. Like what?

JOE DON. Your left breast, it sits higher than the other one.

SHEENA. Surgical error.

JOE DON. I favor irregular.

SHEENA. Adds interest.

JOE DON. I can see that.

SHEENA. What is your major flaw?

JOE DON. Low I.Q. Tested me three times, it went down every time.

SHEENA. My experience is that smart just messes up your instincts.

JOE DON. Little lady, I turn my instincts loose you'd have to call disaster relief.

SHEENA. Ready to go, huh?

JOE DON. Hair trigger.

SHEENA. Doesn't scare me cowboy.

(electric pause)

JOE DON. Well now, Sheila…

SHEENA. Sheena.

JOE DON. I act on my instincts it's pretty much like a hydrogen bomb…Scorched earth thing all the way to the horizon.

SHEENA. I'm slow to burn. *(a pause)* But when I light up, I could cook your tongue.

JOE DON. I figured that. *(They both stare at the floor.)* So.

SHEENA. So.

JOE DON. So.

SHEENA. You want to sit on the sofa with me?

JOE DON. Wouldn't mind.

(They sit side by side just short of touching.)

SHEENA. You put out some serious heat.

JOE DON. Hereditary. My daddy run a hundred and two fever all his life.

SHEENA. How come you only look at me out of the corner of your eye?

JOE DON. Bobcat clawed me. I only got peripheral vision.

SHEENA. If I knew you a hundred years you'd never look straight at me?

JOE DON. No can do.

SHEENA. How would you get to know me?

JOE DON. By touch.

SHEENA. You have a woman at your cabin?

JOE DON. I had one, but she went off lookin' for toilet paper.

SHEENA. Lately?

JOE DON. Three years and some.

SHEENA. It's peaceful?

JOE DON. Grace descending.

SHEENA. Put your arm around me.

JOE DON. Yes ma'am.

(They sit.)

Yeah?

SHEENA. Joe Don…

JOE DON. Yeah?

SHEENA. What's the thing you like best in this world?

JOE DON. Wall-to-wall silence.

(pause)

SHEENA. I like this. Anything we should do?

JOE DON. Let it sink in.

SHEENA. And then what?

JOE DON. Rest easy.

SHEENA. Rest. You know any songs?

JOE DON. Oh, maybe a thousand.

SHEENA. Sing me a song Joe Don.

JOE DON. *(sings 'Streets of Laredo' in a rough and ready tenor)*
When I walked out on the streets of Laredo
When I walked out in Laredo one day,
I spied a young cowboy, all dressed in white linen

*(**SHEENA** puts her head on his shoulder.)*

Dressed in white linen and cold as the clay.

(lights down.)

End of Act One

ACT TWO

Scene One

(The next morning. SHEENA is curled up on the couch in JOE DON's shirt with JOE DON's jacket thrown casually over her. There is a note pinned to it. An odd figure with orange hair peers in the barred window. LOLI unlocks the bedroom door and peers out.)

LOLI. Joe Don?

(The orange haired creature scuttles off.)

Don't jump out at me, Joe Don. *(checks around)* Joe Don? Well what...*(one more look)* Huh, Came and went. Well that's just right in character. Crackly? *(takes note)* Wrote in blood. He's always doin' that. *(reads)* No. Huh-uh. *(to the evaporated JOE DON)* I was really your single, one concern, huh? Ooooooo, that pisses me off. *(phone rings)* Hello Mama, how did I know it was you? From where did Joe Don call you? He tried to drag me is what. Cute? I am not his girl, Mama. Mama, I am holding a note written in his own blood to another woman. He drove all this way, saw her, forgot you, forgot me, got scared of her, run off and now he's probably in some truck stop bar cutting off people's ears. *(listens, then emits strangled cry)* Aaaaaaarrrgghhh. *(removes hand)* I'm not marrying my cousin and have my kids grow up to drool on their banjos...

(SHEENA is having her usual nightmare.)

SHEENA. Get off me, get off me, get off me.

LOLI. Got to go, Mama.

SHEENA. No, no, don't do it.

LOLI. Please don't cry, Mama. *(hangs up)*

SHEENA. Don't inject me with your bug poison. Eeeeee!

LOLI. *(loud and unsympathetic)* Wake up, you're in a nightmare, fool.

SHEENA. Bugs

LOLI. You always got bugs.

SHEENA. These were different bugs.

LOLI. I don't give a cockroach's penis.

SHEENA. Excuse me?

LOLI. You heard me, harlot.

SHEENA. Priscilla… *(realizing **JOE DON** is absent)* Where'd that nihilist go?

LOLI. You tell me?

SHEENA. Are you implying he left Sheena??

LOLI. Yeah, maybe you bored his pants right on.

SHEENA. *(commanding)* Priscilla, get me a moist towelette.

LOLI. Get your own towelette. You are sitting there in his shirt! *(waves note at her)* I don't doubt that you've slept with a thousand men, but I would like a free pass exemption for members of my family.

SHEENA. Oh, I see.

LOLI. Did you sleep with him?

SHEENA. I did, yes.

LOLI. Who told you you could do that!?

SHEENA. As in *Zzzzzz*. He never touched me. He sang me to sleep like a Kobe beef.

LOLI. *(waving note)* If you didn't sleep with him then what's this?

SHEENA. Give me my mail, Priscilla.

LOLI. You get everything there is to get in the universe. You don't need Joe Don.

SHEENA. Why, because you want him?

LOLI. *(furious)* Did I say that? Did you hear me say that? I'm not sitting here in his smelly shirt. I just don't see why you have to have him?

SHEENA. *(smiling)* Because you want him.

LOLI. Do not!

SHEENA. Then hand over the note.

LOLI. You're not getting it.

SHEENA. That is my personal property.

LOLI. If you have to know it's a map to his cabin.

SHEENA. You mean it's my map to his cabin.

LOLI. I don't care.

SHEENA. Then you are a thief, Priscilla. God told you "thou shalt not steal" and you went right ahead and did it.

LOLI. Ahhhhhhhh!

SHEENA. Frankly, God hates you.

LOLI. *(throws note at her)* There, there take it. Why am I forever the prisoner of the Ten Commandments?

SHEENA. *(Picking up the note. Sweetly.)* Because you were born in a red state.

(**LOLI**, *changing her mind, grabs the note back and eats it.*)

What did you just do, Priscilla?

LOLI. I ate the map.

SHEENA. Yes, you did.

LOLI. You wanted the map.

SHEENA. I did, yes. I wanted the map.

LOLI. A sane person doesn't eat a map. I'm going crazy.

SHEENA. You don't understand, I wanted that map!

LOLI. What is it I want?

SHEENA. What everybody wants, power, money, and mangos.

LOLI. I don't know…I don't know, I don't know, I don't know! I just want something.

SHEENA. I want something!

LOLI. But I want something bigger than the something you want!

SHEENA. There is no bigger something than the something I want!!

LOLI. Whatever I want, it seems like you have it, and you keep getting it and there's never any left for me. Heck, I don't want Joe Don. But if I did want him you'd get him anyway and that just pisses me off. *(kicks the bean-bag chair)*

SHEENA. Well nobody gets him; he's disappeared into thin air.

LOLI. But he's my family.

SHEENA. So? Everybody is somebody's family. I hate family.

LOLI. Well family pisses me off but it's the only thing that sticks. I don't want my mama but my mama calls *me*. I don't *want* Joe Don but he drives two thousand miles to get me. What the heck is wrong with me that only what pisses me off wants me?

SHEENA. See now, that is deep Priscilla. That is real. *What* wants me are surfer shark movies and they *piss* me off. Who wants me is twelve year-old girls who think if they get me alone I'd explain what an orgasm is.

LOLI. What is it?

SHEENA. *(continuing)* What you really, truly, deeply want is always bigger than you, deeper than you, stranger than you and is probably the most dangerous, worst thing you could possibly want. Which is why I wanted that map!

LOLI. Joe Don is not the North Star, Crackly. He is inconstant as a pinball. You'd just go up there and then get sent off.

SHEENA. There is not a man born of woman sends Sheena Keener off.

LOLI. Yeah? Well he was born Cesarean. You go up there, he'll move on. You wait here, he won't come back. Mama made him swear to get me, he comes, you scare him off, now he's gone. His compass don't work!

SHEENA. I have an ancient Chinese sexual position that remagnetizes a man's compass.

LOLI. Don't you understand? He never, ever, never backs up. Plus, I don't see you going off and living like a prehistoric cave woman.

SHEENA. Or I could just stay in Hollywood.

LOLI. I would give up eternal life to be something barely noticed in Hollywood.

(The front door is kicked in. A blast of smoke and through the smoke a female creature with orange hair in a vampirish dress with army boots. She carries a boom-box. She speaks in a mixture of English and German.)

STALKER. Tochter der Nacht, *(translation: Daughter of the night,)*

LOLI. Your stalker?

SHEENA. Not again.

STALKER. ...ich komme! *(translation: I come!)*

*(The **STALKER** hits the play button and "The Ride of the Valkyries" fills the air. The **STALKER** drops into a crouch and moves to **SHEENA**. **SHEENA** ad libs "Oh my God," as the **STALKER** moves around her.)*

STALKER. Du bist meine Seelenbraut. Ich brauche dich so wie ich Luft und Wasser brauche. Meine Geliebte. Mir gehoerst du, mir. *(translation: You are my soul mate. I must have you as I have air and water. My Sheena. Mine. Mine.)*

SHEENA. Stop pinching me.

STALKER. Deine Stimme ist Musik fuer mich. *(translation: Your voice is music.)* *(grabs **SHEENA** and wrestles her to the floor)* Du bist mein und ich bin dein. *(translation: You are me and I am you.)*

SHEENA. Get her off me.

LOLI. Oh my Lord...

STALKER. My Sheena...

*(The wild cry of a night bird from the **STALKER**.)*

SHEENA. Off me.

LOLI. Boy, I'm not in Kansas anymore.

SHEENA. She's eating me.

LOLI. No eating, you stop that.

STALKER. I am Sheena.

LOLI. See, that's where you're getting confused.

*(Releasing **SHEENA**, the **STALKER** flies at **LOLI**, shrieking, and grabs her by the hair.)*

Ow! You piss-ant.

(STALKER is dragging LOLI to the door.)

STALKER. Aufgepasst, ihr Kinder der Nacht. Wir kommen, Meister. *(translation: Heed them, Children of the Night. We come, Master.)*

(GALAXY enters.)

GALAXY. Release her, Thing of Darkness!

(STALKER releases LOLI, takes a step toward GALAXY. GALAXY, like a gunfighter, whips out a crucifix.)

STALKER. No, no.

GALAXY. Go spirit of malevolence.

STALKER. Zerrt mich nicht vom Himel herunter. *(translation: Do not drag me down from the heavens.)*

GALAXY. Absent thee from my sight for all eternity.

(Thrusts the crucifix at the STALKER. The STALKER rushes out, growling.)

LOLI. How did you do that?

GALAXY. She's German, she likes to be dominated. *(turning to SHEENA)* Hello Sheena.

LOLI. Say, I know you...

GALAXY. I'm her agent. Nice to see you again.

(Wild animal cries as the creature races back in, grabs the boombox and races out. GALAXY pulls a six pack out of her bag.)

GALAXY. I brought beer. *(slaps it down on table)* You are a bad, bad girl. *(close to SHEENA)* Whoa, that shirt smells. *(pulls summer dress from bag)* Brought you a new ensemble. And pumps. *(tosses it to her)*

LOLI. *(pointing to door)* That thing tried to eat us.

GALAXY. About half the stalkers in Hollywood think they're vampires. *(tosses LOLI a beer)* Have one. This one has her own smoke effects. Makes the Sixties look like the Age of Reason. *(tosses SHEENA a beer)* You look like you could use one. Let's do a little business.

LOLI. Jiminy.

GALAXY. As Sheena knows I am 19 years-old and I am the wiliest, sexiest, most powerful and hated B-list agent in the world, so it is counter-productive to be chasing cinematic shark bait of questionable magnitude into transitional neighborhoods. *(hits wall with show)* Spider. *(wipes it off on sofa)* Sheena, Sheena, Sheena.

LOLI. *(from behind her)* 'Scuse me.

GALAXY. Who precisely is this?

SHEENA. My assistant Priscilla.

GALAXY. You wrecked my office and set wild Dachshunds on me. I can admire that.

LOLI. *(slight curtsey)* Well, thank you. And you're famous, right?

GALAXY. I am Galaxy, bigger than a star.

LOLI. And you are in the movies right?

GALAXY. I am not an actor little wooden head; I am an agent. Do you believe in God?

LOLI. Oh sure.

GALAXY. Well, I'm like God, only more visual; I create the people who are in the movies.

LOLI. You do?!

SHEENA. How did you find me?

GALAXY. I knew where you were every minute, baby.

SHEENA. No, you didn't.

GALAXY. Yeah, I did. During your last surgical tune-up...I had a Global positioning chip implanted in your ear-lobe. **(SHEENA** *touches her left ear.)* Other side baby.

SHEENA. I have to lie down now.

LOLI. 'Scuse me.

GALAXY. What? !

LOLI. Who did you create?

GALAXY. Did I grant you access?! *(answering* **LOLI***'s question)* Chi-Chi Acuna.

LOLI. I love Chi-Chi! You created her?

GALAXY. Discovered Chi-Chi sitting next to me in the 4th grade. Bam! I knew she had "it."

LOLI. What's "it"?

SHEENA. *(on floor)* I'm it.

GALAXY. So, I forged a check on my parents' saving account...

LOLI. You didn't dare!

GALAXY. ...and produced Chi-Chi's legendary videos "Sleepover Sirens" and "Little Strawberry's Paddling Party," which I shot with my little friends while my parents played Scrabble downstairs.

LOLI. Gollee.

    *(**SHEENA** wanders about looking at the walls.)*

GALAXY. *(stops and stares at **LOLI**)* You are fabulously ugly.

LOLI. I am?

GALAXY. It's not just that your looks are below average but that you embody that platonic and Jungian ideal of ugliness, thus anyone shot in the same frame with you would be, by contrast, sublimely beautiful. Perhaps in you I have discovered the touchstone.

LOLI. *(thrilled)* You mean I could be in the movies?

GALAXY. *(stares at **LOLI** again)* No, forget it.

LOLI. But you said...

SHEENA. *(exploding)* How can I be a role model for girls if I get eaten in the first eighteen minutes of the movie?

GALAXY. Sheena...I have explained to you that your erotic fragility, profound neurosis, and damaged angel looks make you the pre-eminent cinematic whore-victim of your era.

SHEENA. I am.

GALAXY. You are the second most popular actress in films among potential suicides under thirty.

SHEENA. *(getting upset)* But Eyes...eyes...I don't want that. *(starts to scratch)*

GALAXY. Focus. Breathe. You have two towering ambitions, to be everything and nothing. Galaxy knows you.

*(**SHEENA** lets out a scream of frustrations and pain. **GALAXY** tosses her a beer.)*

Have another beer.

*(**SHEENA** opens it and chugs it, then she leans against the wall.)*

LOLI. I could make flapjacks.

GALAXY. You make flapjacks?

LOLI. I got batter right in the fridge.

SHEENA. *(wanting attention)* Hey?

GALAXY. I would kill for a flapjack.

LOLI. Really? No kiddin'?

GALAXY. *(to **SHEENA**)* You hear this?

*(**LOLI** heads back to kitchen.)*

Where you from girl?

LOLI. Flatt, Kansas.

GALAXY. You mean two 'T' Flatt, not flat. *(gestures)*

LOLI. *(delighted)* Yeah!

SHEENA. Hey.

GALAXY. That's over by Chanute, right?

LOLI. More toward Winfield.

SHEENA. Sheena needs attention.

GALAXY. *(pointing toward herself)* Saxonburg.

LOLI. I know where that's at!

GALAXY. Shut up! Kansas and Kansas.

SHEENA. I exist.

LOLI. *(puts hand out over kitchen counter)* I'm real honored to meet you.

GALAXY. *(not taking hand)* Flapjacks, baby, the one true religion! *(cracks her third beer)*

LOLI. Coming right out!

SHEENA. I cannot do any of this anymore. *(**GALAXY** focuses on her.)* I can't!

*(**GALAXY** pulls a beautifully, elegantly wrapped package out of her bag. Reads tag.)*

GALAXY. For the goddess Sheena. Come sit by Mommy. Sit! Goodness me, what could this be?

SHEENA. What?

GALAXY. This could be everything my Little Crackly ever wanted in one pretty package.

(SHEENA reaches out.)

No, no, no, don't touch.

(gently brushes SHEENA's hair away from her face)

Galaxy knows you have suffered. Over at the agency I cried for you...yes, tears. So, worried and distraught as I was, I said to myself, Charity...*(amazed, covering her mouth)* Did I just...did you hear me say my birth name that I never, never reveal? But...well the three of us, Charity, Sheena, and whoever the hell you are, we are letting our hair down, bonding...don't you feel that vibe? *(tosses beer can)* Don't you sense our menstrual cycles are locking in? Our rhythm. Beautiful. And I have brought the good news!

(LOLI brings a flapjack over.)

LOLI. You read the Bible?

GALAXY. I cast the Bible. *(indicating the flapjack)* What's that?

LOLI. There's more to come.

GALAXY. Now this is what I'm talking about! Golden brown, crispy edges. And this syrup. Is this homemade?

LOLI. Wild huckleberry from Mama's field patch.

GALAXY. Tangy. I could market this syrup. I want to diversify so I might get into syrup. Yummy, yum, yum.

SHEENA. What good news?

GALAXY. Okay, here's the deal, Sheena. You have to do a play.

SHEENA. Cannot.

GALAXY. Crackly, munchkin, you can do a play, you just can't act. That's perfect. What's acting? The men love you because you get naked with Romeo; the women love you because you're fat.

SHEENA. Fat?!

GALAXY. Don't worry; it's adorable. Bingo! You're back on the radar. Hollywood is galvanized. You're not shark-bait. *(a headline)* You're Broadway!

SHEENA. I *cannot* be looked at. I would run.

GALAXY. Then I would have you killed, wouldn't I? *(eats in high good humor)* This syrup is so cheering me up.

LOLI. You don't mean kill, kill?

GALAXY. Priscilla, Priscilla, Priscilla. You have to follow through. This is fantasy land and one of the few real things is revenge. *(handing plate to LOLI)* And if you're not feared, if it's sensed you can be crossed, that you don't follow through, well then that's blood in the water and what shows up then?

LOLI. Sharks.

GALAXY. Yes, sharks. So if a client, say this client…*(pats SHEENA)* Left me, with a contract in force, what would I have to do to save myself from the… *(points at both LOLI and SHEENA)*

LOLI.	**SHEENA.**
Sharks.	Sharks.

GALAXY. *(triumphant)* I would have to…

LOLI. *(thrilled to know the answer)* Follow through!

SHEENA. *(not so thrilled)* Follow through!

GALAXY. Yes! It's follow-through that makes you distinct. I, Galaxy, give my clients an imaginary identity; I make Sheena distinct and thus you, our ticket buyer, feel distinct in perceiving her.

LOLI. *(beat)* What's in the present?

GALAXY. Neither of you have the faintest idea what I'm talking about, do you? The trouble with genius is that it sounds like bullshit.

LOLI. But what's in the present?

GALAXY. I'll simplify. *(goes to get the last beer)* By disappearing you have freshened up your brand. The media, the bloggers, the tabloid press are panting with suspense! I weave the storyline like a spider. You're gone, story one. You're found, story two. You go immediately into drug treatment, story three…

SHEENA. But I'm not using.

GALAXY. I have hypodermics in my shoulder bag. We have you impregnated by an, as of yet, unspecified rapper, story four.

LOLI. For real?

GALAXY. Now story five, just prior to rehearsing Juliet you are sprung from treatment by armed dwarfs.

LOLI. I love dwarfs!

GALAXY. Rehearsal starts in Verona, Italy – story six. You have an accidental fall from the balcony, story seven, and thus lose the child...

LOLI. No...

GALAXY. ...story eight. By then it's a feeding frenzy. Tickets to the opening are scalped at five thousand dollars! On opening night you faint after your first line, the ceiling opens up and a helicopter whisks you away, and the next day you start shooting the movie.

| **LOLI.** | **SHEENA.** |
| What movie? | What movie? |

GALAXY. Romeo and Juliet. The press crawls to us on their knees!

SHEENA. They did that movie.

GALAXY. *(touching her cheek)* But not the way you'll do it. No one has ever done it the way you'll do it. Open the package.

(SHEENA picks it up.)

GALAXY. *(cont.)* You're the franchise, baby. You, you, it's all you 24/7. Name above the title. It is frantically awaited. We film, we get to the final scene. The tomb. Romeo dead beside you. You reach out...open it.

(SHEENA tears open the package.)

Voila!

SHEENA. It's a dagger.

GALAXY. 17th Century. The real deal.

SHEENA. *(holding it up)* It's beautiful.

GALAXY. Shhh. Rolling. Take one. *(She tosses the beer can, then turns as if the noise startles her.)* "Yea, noise? Then I'll be brief. O happy dagger! *(touches her chest)* This is thy sheath; there rust and let me die." *(mimes stabbing herself)* Bingo. You die at the moment the character dies. It's a wrap. Universal sensation.

LOLI. Ummmm.......

GALAXY. *(raises a fist)* Immortality! We're the most famous film in cinematic history...forever.

SHEENA. Why?

GALAXY. Because you die. We see you die.

SHEENA. Really?

GALAXY. Really.

LOLI. Wait a minute.

SHEENA. Really, really die?

GALAXY. Really die.

LOLI. Yeah, but...

GALAXY. No more eyes. No more pain. Nobody looks at you ever again.

LOLI. 'Scuse me.

GALAXY. Did I promise you? Everything and oblivion simultaneously.

LOLI. But she's dead.

GALAXY. *(irritated)* Priscilla, nothing is free in Hollywood.

SHEENA. No more eyes?

GALAXY. No more eyes.

SHEENA. It's good.

GALAXY. Immortal like a goddess.

(SHEENA nods.)

LOLI. *(upset)* But she's dead.

GALAXY. Crackly has it all. Take my hand sugar.

(SHEENA rises, LOLI goes to the wall and gets the 2x4.)

The greatest of all time.

(LOLI takes it down.)

GALAXY. *(cont.)* We're not going for the easy win, Crackly... *(spreads her arms wide)* We are going for the knockout!

(LOLI whacks GALAXY from behind. GALAXY, pole-axed falls to the floor. A moment.)

LOLI. I just don't like her.

SHEENA. *(aghast)* You hit her with a 2x4.

LOLI. And I followed through!

SHEENA. But why?!

LOLI. First of all she looked straight at me and called me ugly, which is not something you say to a hostess. Second of all, I may be dumb but even I, Crackly, know...what she had in mind for you!

SHEENA. What?

LOLI. It was on her mind to walk you outta here and star your insane self in a snuff film!

SHEENA. *(as if it were logical)* So I wouldn't be looked at.

LOLI. God in heaven woman, if you can't figure out there are a thousand ways not to be looked at that don't include killin' your damn self, then you are just about one nipple shy of a tit!

SHEENA. She said I would be famous and it would be the most famous movie in history.

LOLI. But you wouldn't know it because you would be dead!!

(They look at each other. They turn and look down at GALAXY.)

SHEENA. I'd be dead forever.

LOLI. Yes.

SHEENA. In an urn.

LOLI. Yes.

(a pause)

SHEENA. *(mulling it over)* I don't think I'd like that.

LOLI. No.

SHEENA. No one can look sexy in an urn.

LOLI. That's right.

SHEENA. *(decisive)* So I'm not doing that.

LOLI. Yes!

(They turn to look at GALAXY.)

SHEENA. Is *she* dead?

LOLI. I don't know. She wouldn't be dead. Would she be dead?

SHEENA. Well, find out Priscilla.

(LOLI. goes down on her knees, checks.)

LOLI. I think she's dead; I killed her.

SHEENA. She might be holding her breath!

LOLI. She is not holding her breath! She's not breathing!

SHEENA. Do not shout at me.

LOLI. If she is dead, we are toast.

SHEENA. Toast?

LOLI. We'll be electrified.

SHEENA. They don't do the electric chair in California.

LOLI. Well, that's good.

SHEENA. The Governor comes over to your house and kills you personally.

LOLI. She moved.

SHEENA. She didn't move.

LOLI. Wait. Mama said there is one thing a woman should keep on her person at all *times…a* straight pin.

(She removes one from her dress. SHEENA pulls off one of GALAXY's shoes and holds up her foot. LOLI looks up.)

Thy will be done.

(She rams the pin into GALAXY's foot.)

GALAXY. *(roaring)* BIIIITCHHHH!!!

(She immediately blacks out again. SHEENA and LOLI embrace.)

LOLI. Yes.

SHEENA. Yes!

LOLI. We're saved!

> (**SHEENA** *puts her head in her hands.*)

We're not saved?

SHEENA. She is…Galaxy…She is connected; for what we have done she knows horrible, demon people who will cut our hearts out and eat them.

LOLI. They would?

SHEENA. She is unbelievably savage.

LOLI. We could go to that jungle place.

SHEENA. She will pursue us to the ends of the earth.

LOLI. Wow.

SHEENA. It's hopeless. We have Juliet's dagger; we might just as well finish ourselves off.

LOLI. Well maybe, but see, I got to tell you, I'm having a pretty good time. Before now, well okay, that was a bad time. My daddy running off, gettin' pulled into that police cruiser. Bein' so alone here I just sat around countin' the hairs on my arm. But just since you showed up, I never had so many adventures in my whole life! You all bloody in that beautiful dress, and then, bam, I turned into Priscilla and I hid out from Joe Don and the vampire tried to eat me, and this big time agent busts in and everybody wants flapjacks, and I get into the housewares and syrup business and knock out a Hollywood notable with a 2x4, hell, it was big fun! So, hey, I'm sorry but I'm taking a pass on the dagger.

SHEENA. *(amazed)* You mean you're happy?

LOLI. *(careful)* Well maybe.

SHEENA. I have to lie down on the floor now.

LOLI. Crackly, please, please don't lie down on the floor.

SHEENA. I have to curl up.

LOLI. No. Really, don't curl up on the floor. We have to do somethin'!

SHEENA. I'll just lie down here 'til she wakes up and takes me back.

LOLI. You are not going back!

SHEENA. I could have gone off to the woods with the cowboy...

LOLI. And he's not exactly a cowboy...

SHEENA. *(singing)* "When I walked out in the streets of Laredo"

(a moan from **GALAXY***)*

LOLI. Oh-oh. Okay, okay, we got to take hold here. Ummm, Joe Don could do this. What would Joe Don do? Okay... *(heads for kitchen)* Joe Don likes duct-tape. *(rummages through drawer)* Duct-tape. He runs down a bond jumper, first thing he duct-tapes 'em. *(finds it)* Okay good.

SHEENA. But why?

LOLI. Crackly, I'm kind of running on instincts here.

SHEENA. You can't, for no reason, just duct-tape a Hollywood legend.

LOLI. *(rolling* **GALAXY** *over face down)* Well, I didn't think I could but yippi-ay-a, I'm doin' it. Could you help me!

(tapes **GALAXY***'s hands behind her)*

You know now I think about it, it's a little like the rodeo. I did little league rodeo, you know, where you rope golden retrievers? *(finishes the hands)* Yes! I bet Joe Don just tears this stuff with his teeth. *(She does. It tears.)* Damn, this is good for your sense of self!

SHEENA. *(sitting up, taking control)* Priscilla, I have seen personal assistants run mad.

LOLI. See, but I'm remembering now, I'm not Priscilla.

SHEENA. *(rising)* Stop that this instant!

LOLI. My name is Loli.

SHEENA. Priscilla...

LOLI. Sit down and shut up!

*(***SHEENA** *does.)*

Thank you a bunch. All right now...ummm... *(binding her feet)* And a one, and a two, and a three, and a four. *(looks at her work)* Okay, now then...ummmm...

SHEENA. Now then what?

LOLI. Well, probably...or maybe we should...see, what Joe Don would do...

*(Sits with **SHEENA**. They look at **GALAXY**.)*

I just don't have a single idea in the world.

*(**GALAXY** makes word-like sounds.)*

LOLI. Oh-oh.

GALAXY. Where am I? What is this?

*(She sees **SHEENA** and **LOLI**, issuing something like a low growl.)*

SHEENA.	**LOLI.**
Hi.	Hi.

GALAXY. You have...bound Galaxy and she is...on the floor.

SHEENA.	**LOLI.**
Uh-huh.	Uh-huh.

GALAXY. I...don't...like this!

LOLI. Well, I could get you a nice cold compress for your...

GALAXY. You hit me.

LOLI. *(demonstrates)* I followed through...

GALAXY. You are both going to prison with murderous Hollywood lesbians I represent. But after that, if there is an after that, mysterious fires will break out wherever you live, your pets will die, your plants will go missing, your identities will be stolen.

*(**JOE DON** appears in the doorway, unseen by the others.)*

You will mysteriously gain two hundred pounds, lose all your body hair and crawl on all fours...

*(**JOE DON** neatly inserts a balled-up kerchief in **GALAXY**'s mouth, silencing her, and picks up **SHEENA**.)*

JOE DON. Ma'am.

SHEENA. Wait!

JOE DON. Forgot somethin'.

(exts)

LOLI. Joe Don. Joe Don! Joe Don!!

JOE DON. *(reappearing)* I can't be shooting the breeze; I got things to do.

SHEENA. Put me down!

JOE DON. Yes, ma'am.

SHEENA. And do not call me ma'am. *(back on her feet)*

JOE DON. *(looking down)* Say, who gaffed him up?

LOLI. I did.

JOE DON. That's a real professional job.

LOLI. Thank you.

JOE DON. How come he's dressed up as a girl?

LOLI. What?

SHEENA. She.

JOE DON. He.

SHEENA. She.

JOE DON. He!

SHEENA. She!

JOE DON. Hell, we could settle this easy if we looked up his short shorts but that would be plain rude.

LOLI. Joe Don, you are out of your mind.

JOE DON. Then hand me over his saddlebag there.

*(**LOLI** gives him the bag. He dumps it out. Pill bottles abound. Picks up drivers license.)*

SHEENA. This is Galaxy. She is bigger then a star!

JOE DON. Uh-huh. Driver's license. Nice picture. What's this say here?

SHEENA/LOLI. Charles Chumpé.

JOE DON. Damn, I hate to be right all the time.

LOLI. Charles?

SHEENA. How did you know she was a he, Joe Don?

JOE DON. Girl, I told you about my instincts.

LOLI. I thought her secret name was Charity.

SHEENA. No. It says Charles.

LOLI. That liar.

SHEENA. *(looking at license)* Nooooo, this date can't be right.

LOLI. What?

SHEENA. Birthdate. July 23, 1977. 1970 to 2000 is thirty, minus 7 is….

LOLI. 23.

SHEENA. Plus 8 is…

LOLI. 31.

SHEENA. He is 31 years old! *(astounded)* He could have known Richard Nixon!

(frantic reaction from **GALAXY**)

Everyone thinks she was the youngest power agent in Hollywood. It was her whole thing. She got girl teen because she was girl teen. She *knows*. Everybody bought that. But yo, she's not Galaxy expert on female preteen, she's Charles Chumpé from deepest Kansas and she's not Miss Teen Nineteen, she's some withered old dude!

JOE DON. Yup.

SHEENA. *(locks eyes with* **JOE DON**) I thought you never come back?

JOE DON. Never do.

SHEENA. So what is it you came back to get, cowboy?

JOE DON. What I have to have.

SHEENA. Well?

(A moment pause, then they rocket into an incredibly passionate kiss. It goes on. The phone rings, the kiss intensifies. **LOLI** *picks up.)*

LOLI. Yeah Mama, I figured it might be you.

*(***SHEENA** *leaps up wrapping her legs around* **JOE DON***'s waist. He staggers back against the wall for support.)*

Yeah Mama, Joe Don came back, he forgot something.

(The kiss continues as they crash into a wall.)

I can't talk right now Mama; I'm watchin' pornography. Well, Mama…Well, Mama…

(The kiss continues.)

Mama, it's hard for me to concentrate.

(She hangs up. The kiss devolves onto the floor where it rolls about.)

You stop that!

(JOE DON *and* **SHEENA** *separate with a wild yell. They stay on the floor breathing hard.)*

JOE DON. *(rising)* I beg your pardon, Loli-Elizabeth.

LOLI. Hey, what the hell?

JOE DON. We kind of got tied up in a big hello.

LOLI. I could see that.

JOE DON. You look a little sour.

LOLI. You look a little winded.

JOE DON. You weren't sweet on me were you Loli Elizabeth?

LOLI. About as much as I'd like to suck spit from a gerbil.

JOE DON. 'Cause you'd need a *good* person.

LOLI. You could be.

JOE DON. Not in my DNA darlin'. Smell me. Go on.

(LOLI *takes a whiff and makes a face.)*

See, that is the acid test. I'm the last damn thing on this wrecked up planet you want to get tangled up with. Okay?

LOLI. Okay. Forget it.

JOE DON. Damn good choice.

LOLI. I…I'm sorry I shot at you.

JOE DON. Always take that as a compliment.

SHEENA. Hey!

(JOE DON *turns.)*

You smell like dirt and hot sauce.

JOE DON. Much obliged.

(**LOLI** *moves off to kitchen, gets a Big Red, watches.*)

SHEENA. Where you live is empty, right cowboy?

JOE DON. Give or take a little wildlife.

SHEENA. Quiet?

JOE DON. You can hear your skin slough off.

SHEENA. How would we be Joe Don?

JOE DON. Tight.

SHEENA. For how long?

JOE DON. Why do you ask?

SHEENA. You have a reputation.

JOE DON. Had the same dog thirteen years.

SHEENA. I've been disappointed in my life Joe Don.

JOE DON. Well that stops here. Period. End.

SHEENA. So you say.

LOLI. Well, I'll say he did come back.

SHEENA. I need a sign Joe Don.

JOE DON. You mean like the heavens open up and the seven horned beast of the millennium rides down on a ray of light and burns my initials on your thigh?

SHEENA. Just an everyday sign.

JOE DON. I filled the back of my truck up with mangos.

SHEENA. *(smiles)* Nice touch.

JOE DON. Deal?

SHEENA. Deal. (**SHEENA** *moves over above* **GALAXY**.) Charity Charles Chumpé, you suck.

JOE DON. Whoa.

SHEENA. You have used me and abused me, turned me into glorified sharkbait, and set me up for a snuff film without even talking to me about billing! One thing though, Charity-Charles: I leave you to be "Galaxy-bigger-than-a-star" but I have here your certified driver's license and if you ever, ever bother me or my loyal assistant Priscilla or Joe Don Carfleck my Prince of Darkness, I will release this license and pop your career like a hot-air balloon.

(GALAXY makes strangled sounds.)

LOLI. What about the chip in your ear?

JOE DON. I'm good with ears.

SHEENA. Goodbye, Galaxy. *(turns to LOLI)* You have been the best of all my Priscillas, Priscilla. As I don't believe I will need an assistant in the wilderness, I now set you free. *(touches the top of her head)* Consider yourself emancipated.

LOLI. Thank you, thank you far a real day in Hollywood.

(Holds out her hand. They shake.)

SHEENA. *(takes her necklace off)* You know what? This is my first tooth on here. Left it for the Tooth Fairy but she never showed up. Maybe it will bring you luck.

LOLI. *(puts it around her neck)* I'd be real proud to wear your tooth.

(LOLI and SHEENA hug.)

JOE DON. Let's roll, woman. There's a vampire stealing mangos off my truck.

LOLI. Now listen Joe Don.

JOE DON. Loli Elizabeth.

LOLI. I just can't…

JOE DON. *(chuckles)* I see what you're after here, girl. Lot a time the journey sucks but you got to take the ride.

LOLI. I do.

JOE DON. Tell your mama anything?

LOLI. Tell her she was right about the straight pin. *(points at GALAXY)* And take him out of here. I'm not running a hotel.

JOE DON. Where to?

LOLI. Maybe stick her in that revolving door in front of his office space.

JOE DON. Don't ordinarily deliver packages, but I'm a fool for love. *(hoists a protesting GALAXY up on his shoulders)* You ready? *(GALAXY subsides.)*

SHEENA. *(to* **LOLI***)* Uh huh. You wish on that tooth, girl-friend.

LOLI. Thank you.

SHEENA. Yubba. *(at door)* Now you see me.

JOE DON. Now you don't.

> **(SHEENA** *takes* **JOE DON***'s hand and they exit.* **LOLI** *is alone. Looks around.)*

LOLI. Well shoot. *(kicks the beanbag)* Lonely in here. I don't know, I don't know, I don't know. I got to get goin' on life. *(while opening the last fortune cookie)* Come on fortune cookie. *(reads fortune)* 'You need electrolysis.' *(rips it and stomps it)* What the hell kind of fortune cookie is that?

> *(Phone rings. She regards it and then rips it out of the wall.)*

Bye Mama.

> **(LOLI** *looks at the destroyed phone in her hand.)*

I am NOT going back to Flatt.

> *(Tosses it onto beanbag. Fingers the necklace* **SHEENA** *gave her.)*

LOLI. *(cont.)* Help me tooth.

> *(There is a knock on the front door jam.)*

Hello?

> *(another knock)*

You may not come in here if you're all bloody.

> *(Opens door, a young woman is revealed.)*

Well...hi.

BEVERLY. Hi. Could I...Could I step in for just a minute?

LOLI. *(backing up two steps)* Okay

BEVERLY. *(moves just inside the door)* Thank you.

LOLI. Okay.

BEVERLY. I'm Beverly Saitou.

LOLI. I'm Loli.

BEVERLY. I know. One moment. *(She speaks Japanese into the cell phone.)* Hai watashi yo. Hai, ima Loli ni hanashite iru no. Ima shita ho ga ii n ja nai? *(translation: "Yes, I'm here. Yes, I'm speaking to Loli now. You should make the celebration now." In response horns blare up and down the street outside.)*

That's my father Masaru, my uncle Kobayashi, my other uncle Nobu and our friend Takumi Itou, all landscape gardeners. They're blowing their horns in the pickup trucks all up and down your street.

LOLI. How come is that?

BEVERLY. For you. Because you fix their trucks. My father says you are very important to our family. When Mr. Johnston sends you away, my father organizes and then 40, 50 trucks block his garage. Then there's a crowd and journalists. Mr. Johnston is very intelligent. He knows what is bad for business. He and my father talk. They shake hands.

*(hands **LOLI** an envelope)*

BEVERLY. *(cont.)* Mr. Johnston writes this letter to ask you to please return. Monday, he says, would be a good time. Would you consider this?

*(**LOLI** nods.)*

That is very, very cool. *(hands out a scroll)* My father sends this gift. *(unrolls it)* He makes this copy of "Chou Mao Su Admiring the Lotus Flowers" by Kano Masanobu. You know Masanobu?

*(**LOLI** shakes her head.)*

He is very great. My dad worked at night for eight years to make the perfect copy.

*(**LOLI** takes it and looks at the scroll.)*

You like it?

LOLI. I sure do.

BEVERLY. Masanobu for him is irreplaceable…and you are irreplaceable he says.

LOLI. Wow.

BEVERLY. *(smiling)* I must go. One more thing. *(speaks into the cellphone in Japanese)* Hanabi shiyo yo.

(translation: "It is time for the fireworks." Fireworks go off. We see them above the set.)

LOLI. What's that?

BEVERLY. Fireworks, for you, in celebration.

LOLI. I just…I don't…you thank your daddy for me. *(looks at scroll)* This is real big for me. You tell him I'll be there on Monday.

BEVERLY. He will be very pleased. *(kisses **LOLI** on cheek)* Bye Loli.

LOLI. Bye Beverly.

*(**BEVERLY** goes. **LOLI** looks at the scroll.)*

Chou Mao Su Admiring the Lotus Flowers.

*(The fireworks continue. We hear music and the building sound of applause. The set melts away. **LOLI** is standing in front of the Hollywood hills twinkling with lights. In the background, the iconic "Hollywood" sign. A podium rises up in front of her. Cheers and applause.)*

LOLI. Golly. Holy moly. Boy, I never…nobody ever…Thank you, thank you…boy, I never ever thought I'd get this. Whoa baby. I'm really, really sorry I don't have any cleavage. This here is my first 'Lotus' award. My first award period. Well, I got one for citizenship in second grade but they took it back. Wow. I want to thank my Mama who always means really well by me even if she can't do it right. And well, okay, my daddy for that time he made me a hill. And I'd like to thank my agent Charley Chumpé, the first one to call me a "touchstone," she couldn't be here; she's in a revolving door…and I especially want to thank my very, very best friend Sheena Keener, who disappeared recently. *(holds scroll over her head)* Wherever you are, Crackly. And Joe Don Stonewall Carfleck who broke my heart in a good way. He's serious family.

(Lush music rises under her speech.)

Oh-oh, got to go. Thank you Beverly and your family for nominating me...and all of you out there, my wonderful fans, who came out tonight to see me, Loli, get this beautiful scroll. *(steps downstage)* Thank you! See you all. See you all at work on Monday! Bye now. Bye now. Bye. Bye.

(She waves and waves, enfolded by applause.)

(lights out)

End of Play

Also by
Jane Martin...

Anton in Show Business

The Boy Who Ate the Moon

Cementville

Criminal Hearts

Cul De Sac

Flags

Flaming Guns of the Purple Sage

Good Boys

Jack and Jill

Keely and Du

Middle Aged White Guys

Mr. Bundy

Sez She

Shasta Rue

Summer

Talking With...

Travellin' Show

Vital Signs

Please visit our website **samuelfrench.com** for complete
descriptions and licensing information.

OTHER TITLES AVAILABLE FROM SAMUEL FRENCH

ANTON IN SHOW BUSINESS

Jane Martin

Full Length, Comedy / 6f / Unit Set

This madcap comedy follows three actresses across the footlights, down the rabbit hole and into a strangely familiar Wonderland that looks a lot like American theatre the resemblance is uncanny! As these women pursue their dream of performing Chekhov in Texas, they're whisked through a maelstrom of "good ideas" that offer unique solutions to the Three Sister's need to have life's deeper purpose revealed. In the tradition of great backstage comedies, Anton in Show Business conveys the joys, pains and absurdities of "putting on a play" at the turn of the century.

**Winner of the 2001 American Theatre Critics
Steinberg New Play Award**

"A smart, acerbic crowd pleaser.... Simultaneously a love letter and a poison pen letter to the American theatre."
– *Variety*

"Funny, smart, wry and poignant."
– *Miami Herald*

"Consciously an example of the problem it addresses, often with aching hilarity, that the world of theatre is growing ever more estranged from the straightforward business of telling stories."
– *The New York Times*

GOOD BOYS

Jane Martin

Full Length, Drama / 5m / Ext.

A fierce encounter between fathers, one black and one white, opens a deeply disturbing chapter in their lives. The men relive the school shooting in which their sons died, one a victim and the other the shooter. When racial issues threaten to derail all hope for understanding and forgiveness, the black father's other son takes matters into his owns hands. He pushes the confrontation to a dangerous and frightening climax. *Good Boys* explores the pressures of modern family life and the breaking points of men and boys, and it raises the question: To what extent are parents responsible for their children's behavior? This topical drama by the author of *Keely and Du* premiered at the Guthrie Theater in Minneapolis.

"Galvanizing."
– *St. Paul Pioneer*

"A terrifying, terrific piece of theatre that is as memorable as it is unsettling."
– *Star Tribune*

OTHER TITLES AVAILABLE FROM SAMUEL FRENCH

FLAGS

Jane Martin

Full Length, Drama / 6m, 2f, extras / Unit Set

This fierce new drama by the author of *Talking With, Anton in Show Business* and *Keely and Du* redefines patriotism as it brings the tragic fallout from the war in Iraq home to America's heartland. When a grieving father inverts our nation's most revered symbol, the family is swept into the vortex of a chaotic war machine. Portrayed in the press as both 'heroes with a cause' and 'enemies of the state,' they become embedded in a bitter struggle for their very survival. Jane Martin gives voice to the white-hot rage and sorrow of our time, delivering a shock-and-awe display of theatrical force.

"...a powerful gut-punch of a play, blisteringly contemporary."
– *Minneapolis Pioneer Press*

"Powerfully mines heartbreak, loss, and disillusion to universalize the Iraq war. Brave, deeply compassionate, and, most importantly, very good drama."
– *Minneapolis City Pages*